DODD, MEAD WONDERS BOOKS include WONDERS OF:

BADGERS. Lavine
CATTLE. Scuro
CORALS AND CORAL REEFS.
    Jacobson and Franz
COYOTES. Lavine
CROWS. Blassingame
DAIRY CATTLE. Scuro
DONKEYS. Lavine and Scuro
DRAFT HORSES. Lavine and Casey
DUST. McFall
EAGLE WORLD. Lavine
EGRETS, BITTERNS, AND
    HERONS. Blassingame
ELEPHANTS. Lavine and Scuro
FLIGHTLESS BIRDS. Lavine
FROGS AND TOADS. Blassingame
GEESE AND SWANS. Fegely
GIRAFFES. Lavine
GOATS. Lavine and Scuro
HIPPOS. Lavine
LIONS. Schaller
MARSUPIALS. Lavine
MICE. Lavine

MULES. Lavine and Scuro
PEACOCKS. Lavine
PIGS. Lavine and Scuro
PONIES. Lavine and Casey
RACCOONS. Blassingame
RATTLESNAKES. Chace
RHINOS. Lavine
SEA HORSES. Brown
SEALS AND SEA LIONS. Brown
SHARKS. Blassingame
SHEEP. Lavine and Scuro
SNAILS AND SLUGS. Jacobson and
    Franz
SPONGES. Jacobson and Pang
TURKEYS. Lavine and Scuro
TURTLE WORLD. Blassingame
WILD DUCKS. Fegely
WOODCHUCKS. Lavine
WORLD OF BEARS. Bailey
WORLD OF HORSES. Lavine and
    Casey
ZEBRAS. Scuro

Wonders of DAIRY

CATTLE

Vincent Scuro

Illustrated with photographs and old prints

DODD, MEAD & COMPANY   New York

To Tina,
who encouraged me to write another book

Illustrations courtesy of: The American Guernsey Cattle Club, 11 *bottom*, 25 *right*, 58; The American Jersey Cattle Club, Columbus, OH, 19, 52; American Milking Shorthorn Society, Springfield, MO, 27; Ayrshire Breeder's Association, Brandon, VT, 56, 57 *top*; Borden, Inc., 60; Brown Swiss Cattle Breeder's Association, Beloit, WI, 6, 12, 25 *top*, 57 *bottom*; Friendship Food Products, Inc., Art Goldman, Maspeth, NY, 51; The Holstein-Friesian Association of America, Brattleboro, VT, 15; Tina Krettecos, 61; National Archives, 9, 11 *top*, 16, 17, 26, 31 *top*, 39, 40, 41 *top*, 44; The Royal Jersey Agricultural and Horticultural Society, Jersey, Channel Islands, 23; Vincent Scuro, 21; United Nations, 36; UNPDAC/Thailand, 41 *middle*; USDA Photo, 33 *top*, 43 *bottom*; USDA Photo by Robert Bjork, 47; USDA Photo by Michelle Bogre, 53; USDA Photo by Don Breneman, 35 *top*; USDA Photo by Dave Brill, 48; USDA Photo by Dana Downie, 31 *bottom*; USDA Photo by Betsy Frampton, 13; USDA Photo by Charles O'Rear, 41 *bottom*; USDA Photo by George A. Robinson, 30 *bottom*; USDA Photo by Byron Schumaker, 18; USDA Photo by Dave Warren, 43 *top*; USDA-SCS Photo, 2-3, 35 *bottom*; USDA-Soil Conservation Service Photo by Erwin W. Cole, 30 *top*, 33 *bottom*; Vermont Travel Division, 37.

1 2 3 4 5 6 7 8 9 10

Library of Congress Cataloging-in-Publication Data

Scuro, Vincent.
  Wonders of dairy cattle.

  Includes index.
  Summary: Examines the breeds, breeding, care, and products of dairy cattle and identifies some famous cows.
  1. Dairy cattle—Juvenile literature. [1. Dairy cattle. 2. Cows] I. Title.
SF208.S356 1986   636.2   85–29394
ISBN 0–396–08783–3

Frontispiece: Holstein cattle grazing on grass and clover in a Montana pasture

Contents

A warm, sweet-scented moment for this Brown Swiss and friends

1

Introducing Dairy Cattle

The cow has been called "Nature's own milk factory." However, cows are not the only milk producers. All female mammals,
including humans, have the ability to produce milk. Buffalo,
donkeys, goats, reindeer, sheep, and dozens of other animals
are milked by Man. Yet cows are by far the greatest suppliers,
providing over ninety percent of the world's milk. In fact, when
people talk about milk, they are usually referring to the milk of
the cow.

Cows raised mainly for their milk are known as dairy cattle.
But not all dairy cattle are cows. Cow is the name given to a
mature female. A mature male is called a bull. The offspring of
a cow and a bull is known as a calf until it is a year old, at which
time it becomes a yearling. A heifer is any cow under three
years of age that has not yet produced a calf. A cow that has
been bred, yielded a calf, and has a good milk-production record
is said to be a mature milker.

Zoologists (scientists who study animals) have placed cattle
in the Bovidae family, a large grouping that includes sheep,

goats, bison, and buffalo. Within Bovidae, cattle belong to the Bovinae subfamily. As a result, they are often referred to as bovines.

Cattle also belong to a subdivision of Bovinae, the *Bos* genus. *Bos* is divided into smaller groups called species. There are two species of cattle. *Bos taurus* is found primarily in North and South America, Europe, and Australia. *Bos indicus*, also called the zebu, lives primarily in Asia, the Middle East, and parts of Africa.

While all cows are potential milk suppliers, some do it better than others. Selective mating of bovines has resulted in the development of breeds with the ability to produce large quantities of high-quality milk. Many of the names given to these breeds, including Holstein-Friesian, Jersey, Guernsey, and Ayrshire, are derived from their geographic origins. Other names, like the Milking Shorthorn, are based on a physical trait. Still others, such as the Brown Swiss and Red Danish, combine appearance with origin.

A purebred has both the characteristics of a certain breed and a documented ancestry. Registered purebreds have had their heritage recorded with a breed association. Cows known as "grades," which comprise the vast majority of all dairy cattle, have most of the characteristics of a particular breed but are ineligible for registration because one of the parents was not a purebred.

Individual cows are known by a variety of names. Some have titles consisting of two to four words with a number. Kinsdale Lady Elegance 42d 373844, Korncrest Buzzy 377669, and Arbor Rose Mac Ruby 174924 are a few examples. Many cows are given "people" names, such as Bessie, Gertrude, Violet, or Beulah. Others have traditional "cow" names like Buttercup, Flower, Bluebell, or Bossy, the last derived from the *Bos* genus.

Dairying is the branch of agriculture dealing with milk pro-

In this 1931 photo, purebred Jerseys grace property of a Maine farmer.

duction. In addition to describing the usage of certain cattle, the term "dairy" is applied to all of the products made from milk. A dairy is a farm devoted chiefly to the production of milk and the manufacture of milk products, such as butter and cheese. A girl or woman who works in a dairy is called a dairymaid. Although "dairyman" originally referred to anyone engaged in this business, the term now means the owner or manager of a dairy.

It's hard to believe that *Eotragus*, a slender, antelope-like creature that roamed the forests of Asia about 25 million years ago, is the original ancestor of the modern dairy cow. *Eotragus* barely produced enough milk to feed its own offspring. Another ancient relative, *Bos primigenius*, an extinct species known as the aurochs, was originally hunted for its meat and skin. As soon as Man realized that he could obtain milk from these beasts as well, he began to capture and tame them.

How early cattle were domesticated is unknown. It is generally acknowledged that their ability to survive on a variety of foods, natural herding instinct, and friendly disposition made the task a relatively simple one. Similarly, the exact date is not known. It is believed that the first domestication occurred between 6000 and 4000 B.C.

Where dairy cattle were first domesticated is known. Archaeologists (students of prehistoric cultures) believe that the early peoples of Egypt, India, and what is now called Iraq were the first cattle raisers. Wild bovines were not captured and tamed in Europe until about 1500 B.C. There were no cattle, wild or tame, in the Western Hemisphere until the late fifteenth century A.D., when Christopher Columbus brought them with him on his second voyage.

Dairy cattle have always been highly prized. Kings awarded vast tracts of land or money to the owners of great milk producers. Nations have passed laws prohibiting the exportation of purebreds or the importation of mixed stock. The former was a way of hoarding valuable animals; the latter of maintaining the purity of a nation's breeds.

Bovines have also been a symbol of wealth. In some modern African societies, these animals are used as money. The dowry of a bride-to-be is often paid in cattle. The more attractive the bride, the higher her price tag in cows! Even the word "cattle" connotes wealth. It is thought to be derived from *catel* and *chattel*, which refer to forms of property.

As noted, cows were not always the efficient milk producers they are today. Better breeding, feeding, and management all have contributed to the increased output. A few centuries ago, it took about ten cows to supply milk for one family. Since 1945, milk yield per animal has more than doubled. Today, one cow can provide enough milk for about ten families!

Milk right out of the cow consists of butterfat suspended in a solution containing lactose (a sugar), proteins, and mineral salts. Water comprises more than eighty percent of cow's milk.

Compare the Guernsey in the 1940's Wisconsin photo above to the improved Guernsey at right.

Production by an individual cow is usually described in terms of milk and butterfat. Cows that yield less butterfat generally produce more milk, and vice versa. Incidentally, output is typically expressed by weight in pounds, not by volume. Two pounds of milk are slightly less than a quart.

The production of milk is a complex process involving many of a cow's systems. It starts with reproduction. Milk cannot be produced until the first calf is born. A cow is generally milked for about ten months after this event, followed by a "drying off" period prior to the birth of the next calf.

Cows rest and chew the cud during the hot afternoon.

Digestion also plays a major role. Cattle, like other members of the Bovidae family, are ruminants or "cud chewers." All ruminants have a digestive system consisting of a stomach with four chambers. Food is only partially chewed in the mouth. Then it is swallowed, passing to the first two chambers, where micro-organisms and enzymes soften it into a small wad. The cud, as it is called, is then coughed back up to the mouth for more chewing. Once this is done, the cud is swallowed again and passed into the second two stomach chambers. Then it is reduced to a pulp that can be digested easily in the intestines. This digestive system not only allows cattle to eat large amounts of coarse, fibrous food but also permits them to graze during the cool of the morning and relax and rechew in the hot afternoon.

Cows consume an incredible amount of food each day. The typical daily diet consists of ten to twelve pounds of hay, fifteen to twenty pounds of grain, and almost fifty pounds of silage, plus twenty-five to fifty gallons of water! About half of the

Opposite: Brown Swiss leads Holstein cows along a Virginia road. Note the barns on the left, and the huge silos for holding silage.

nutrients in the food cows eat goes to their body maintenance. The other half is used to produce milk.

It takes about two days for a cow's body to turn feed into milk. Protein, fatty acids, vitamins, minerals, and water from digested food are transported through the blood to the cow's udder, a huge gland containing tiny sacks called alveoli. There are about a million alveoli per square inch of udder.

An udder can weigh twenty-five to sixty pounds. Weight varies with the cow's age, the amount of milk present, and other factors. Since the actual formation of milk takes place in the alveoli, cows with large udders are preferred.

The main difference between dairy and beef cattle is the development of the udder in females and the amount of flesh on males. Dairy bulls are not as fleshy as their beef counterparts, while the udder of a dairy cow is a great deal larger than that of a female bred for beef.

2

Breeding Dairy Cattle

It is generally agreed that there are three reasons for breeding dairy cattle. One is to increase the size of a herd. Another is to produce milk. The third is to obtain the "ideal" cow or bull by improving the stock.

Nature's method of improving animals is called natural selection. This is often referred to as "survival of the fittest," the belief that only the best, fastest, strongest, most cunning, and rugged survive. The weak, the slow, and the stupid do not.

For centuries, Man has been improving species that have already been through thousands of years of natural selection. During the domestication of livestock, individuals best suited to a particular purpose were chosen for their desirable characteristics and mated. This practice evolved into the science of breeding, which centers around the selection and development of animals that consistently transmit good qualities to their offspring.

If you asked a group of dairy farmers from different parts of the world to describe the ideal dairy cow, they'd probably include a number of desirable qualities. Good health, an even

Artist's rendering of the "ideal" Holstein-Friesian

disposition, and production of milk on a continuous basis would be important. The ability to give birth to many offspring and to transmit desirable characteristics to them would be essential.

The ideal dairy cow would be large, weighing more than 1200 pounds. She would also have a long, wide, moderately deep udder, soft and elastic in texture but close to the body to make it less susceptible to injury. She would be well balanced, with a head of medium length and a broad muzzle. The back would be relatively straight from the withers (highest point of the shoulder) to the top of the tail. A level rump with good width at the hips, and legs that are fairly wide apart would be desirable. Furthermore, she would have soft, loose, and fairly thin skin and be free from the excess fat typical of beef cows.

A description of the ideal dairy bull would include a well-balanced body with a masculine head, a straight back, and a long, level rump. The legs would be straight, medium in length, and squarely placed, with feet that are short and well rounded.

15

This New York State Holstein bull of the 1930's came close to the ideal.

"Beefiness" would be undesirable. Naturally, he would be able to transmit only his best characteristics to his offspring.

The animals described above do not exist yet. But there may come a time in the not so distant future when the ideal becomes a reality.

Improvement of diary cattle stock by developing top-quality animals is the job of master breeders. These men and women focus on maximizing milk yield, increasing the number of offspring a cow produces in her lifetime, and refining desirable physical characteristics.

It has been said that "to breed good dairy cattle is to create." Master breeders "create" by employing several breeding techniques.

Grading up (the practice of using a registered purebred sire with any cow) passes the father's desirable features to his offspring. Crossbreeding (the mating of a male of one breed to females of another) generally results in the transfer of the best traits of both parents to their daughters and sons. However, there is always a risk when crossbreeding, since the breeder never knows what the results will be.

To bring out certain features, breeders use other techniques.

Outbreeding is the mating of cattle of the same breed that have no common ancestors. Inbreeding involves mating close relatives such as sisters and brothers. Line breeding also involves relatives, but these are usually no closer than first cousins.

As noted, the vast majority of people who engage in dairy-cattle breeding do so to increase the size of their herds and to supply milk for commercial markets. Typically, their cows are grades or unregistered purebreds.

Many of the top sires in the United States, Canada, Australia, and the British Isles are used to breed ten to twenty thousand cows a year. Bulls selected as breeding stock have a proven record of fathering healthy and productive offspring. In order to evaluate a particular bull's performance, statistics on milk production by his daughters are gathered over a period of time and compared to the records of all other cows in a herd. This

The services of this "community" Guernsey bull were shared by the cows of the local farmers in North Carolina circa 1928—"grading up."

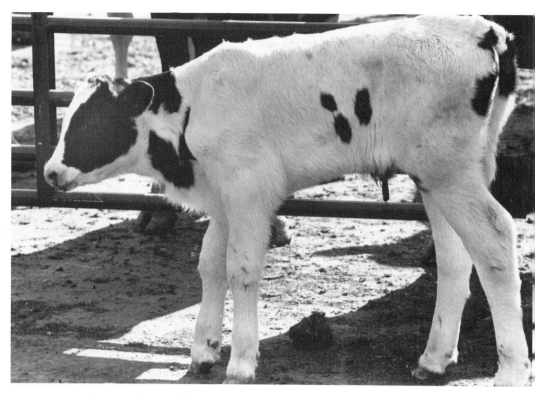

A Holstein calf named Nancy

is called "herdmate comparison." The term "repeatability" is used to describe a bull's ability to sire outstanding daughters on a regular basis.

By nature, animals have their young in the spring, taking advantage of the nice weather and lush pastures of the season. To a dairy farmer, however, a flood of spring-born calves means a surplus of milk, lower prices, and loss of income. As a result, breeding of individuals in a herd is staggered over a period of time.

Once pregnant, a female bovine is known as a bred cow. The gestation period is about 280 days. Most births take place without complications, especially if the cow has had one or more calves already. Some births occur prematurely, and the calf does not live. If the calf survives but the mother doesn't, the newborn is given to a brood cow or "broody" (a female that has recently given birth). On large dairy farms, calves spend their early days in a special section called the calf nursery.

A newborn calf is nourished on colostrum, a milky substance secreted by its mother after the birth. Colostrum contains important ingredients that help the new arrival fight diseases. In a short time, a nursing calf is taught to drink milk from a pail and, for the next three months, is given whole milk. Then it is weaned and fed fodder (coarse vegetation used as food) or grain.

The number of females born each year is about equal to the number of males. Most dairy farmers and breeders dream of altering the ratio of males to females. Farmers who raise cows as milk producers would love to have more heifer calves. Breeders who provide the services of their stock as sires would prefer more bull calves.

A Jersey calf

3

Breeds of Dairy Cattle

Cattle of many breeds come close to achieving the "ideal." A breed is comparable to a human family. All members of a breed have common ancestors. They also have similar characteristics. "Character" (or breed character) refers to the physical features that distinguish one breed from another.

Registered purebred cows of several breeds have been bred specifically for milk production and are most often preferred by dairy farmers. Opinions about which is the best breed of dairy cattle are about as common as flies in a barnyard. Claims of one breed's superiority over another's usually are based more on the enthusiasm of the breeders than on scientific fact. If there *were* a best breed, it would have been discovered years ago and everyone would be raising it to the exclusion of all others!

Here are some of the most widely known dairy breeds.

HOLSTEIN-FRIESIAN. Historians say that early descriptions of these animals erroneously carried the name "Holstein," which is a province in Germany that has no connection with the breed's origins. The "Friesian" part of the name is derived from

A future farmer proudly displays his young Holstein.

a province in the northern part of The Netherlands where much of the early breeding took place. In Canada, Great Britain, and European countries, these dairy cattle are known as Friesians. In the United States, where they dominate the dairy industry, the Holstein name prevails.

Holstein-Friesians are easily identified because they are the only black-and-white breed of dairy cattle. Markings are sharply defined, with differing proportions of each color. A long body and broad hips are common. Cows weigh an average of 1500 pounds; bulls 2200 pounds or more.

Holstein-Friesian cows typically yield over 15,000 pounds of milk per year—more than any other breed. Since they thrive in cold climates, they are preferred by many farmers.

JERSEY. This breed is named for Jersey, one of the islands in the English Channel. Although the inhabitants send many commodities to other countries, the island's best known export is Jersey cattle.

Jerseys have been spread throughout the world. The export of this breed to England, where it is known as the Alderney, has occurred since the late eighteenth century. The first Jerseys arrived in the United States in 1850, when "Mr John A. Tainter imported cattle from the Island paying £18 to £25 for the very best in Jersey." Australia and New Zealand rely heavily on this breed for butter production.

India has imported Jersey bulls and crossed them with females of their own Gir breed. The offspring produce three times as much milk as native stock. The Jamaican Hope, which is popular in tropical regions, is ninety percent Jersey blood. Indeed, the list of countries with Jersey herds grows every year.

Although this breed has been exported around the world, the importation of live cattle into the Island of Jersey has been forbidden since 1763. The law was originally designed to protect Jersey farmers from the competition of imports. Today, it keeps the breed pure.

Jerseys vary from light fawn to almost black, with white, gray, brown, or black spots on some individuals. The head of the typical Jersey has a marked "dish" between the eyes. Some specimens have horns that are forward curving and turned in.

Above: Merlin of Oak Farm 0447, a Jersey bull

Below: A registered purebred Jersey cow

Cows, which weigh about 1000 pounds, have a well-formed udder. Bulls average close to 1500 pounds.

Jerseys are known for producing rich milk that is high in butterfat. Females are easily managed and thus are commonly kept by one-cow families.

GUERNSEY. Another of the Channel Islands, Guernsey lends its name to a breed of dairy cattle. This breed is believed to have originated in the tenth century when French monks brought cattle of the Froment de Leon and Isigny breeds to the tiny island and allowed them to mix. The first Guernseys entered the United States in 1830.

Guernseys are yellowish, brownish, or reddish fawn. White markings are common. Horns, where present, are forward curving and tapered. Cows and bulls weigh about 1100 and 1700 pounds respectively.

Many consider the Guernsey to be the ideal family cow. Mature milkers yield large quantities of whole milk and cream, with enough skim milk left over to feed other livestock such as pigs or chickens. A Guernsey also produces more than fourteen tons of manure each year. That's a lot of fertilizer!

BROWN SWISS. The Brown Swiss is believed to be descended from cattle used in the valleys and mountain slopes of Switzerland during the prehistoric era. As there is little evidence of crossing with other strains, its bloodline is considered to be one of the purest.

The best of the breed are believed to come from Switzerland's Canton of Schwyz, from which the "Swiss" part of the name is derived.

The first part of the breed's name is also appropriate. Brown Swiss are brown. Shadings of color vary from light to dark on individuals and from one member of the breed to another. The hoofs are typically black, the horns white with black tips. Cows weigh about 1400 pounds, while bulls average close to 2000.

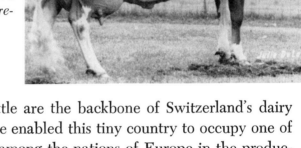

Above: Kilravock Snow-storm, Brown Swiss cow.

Right: Yellow Creek Choice Blossom, a pure-bred Guernsey cow.

Brown Swiss cattle are the backbone of Switzerland's dairy industry. They have enabled this tiny country to occupy one of the highest places among the nations of Europe in the production of milk, cheese, and other dairy products.

The first Brown Swiss cattle in the United States belonged to Henry M. Clark of Belmont, Massachusetts, who imported one bull and seven females during the winter of 1869–70. In the hundred years that followed, only about 25 males and 130 females have entered the country. More than 800,000 Brown Swiss cattle registered in the United States and located in all fifty states are their descendants.

The Brown Swiss cow is popular with owners of small farms throughout the world because it produces about 12,000 pounds of milk per year and does not require a great deal of care.

ARYSHIRE. The highlands in the county of Ayr in Scotland are the ancestral home of the Ayrshires. They were first recognized as a distinct breed sometime prior to 1800. In 1822, they were imported to the United States by H. W. Hills. Today, this breed is well established in every state.

Ayrshires are red or brown and white spotted, with varying amounts of each on individual animals. For many years, the Ayrshire horns were a prominant characteristic of the breed. Today, almost all Ayrshire calves have their horns removed. Ayrshire cows, which weigh about 1200 pounds, have a well-formed udder and lean body structure. The average weight for bulls is about 1850 pounds.

Like Guernseys and Jerseys, Ayrshires are often used by single-cow families as a reliable source of milk and manure.

An Ayrshire cow on a New Hampshire farm, circa 1926

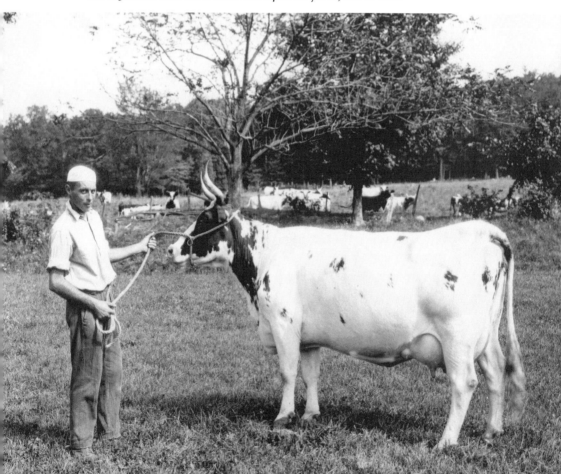

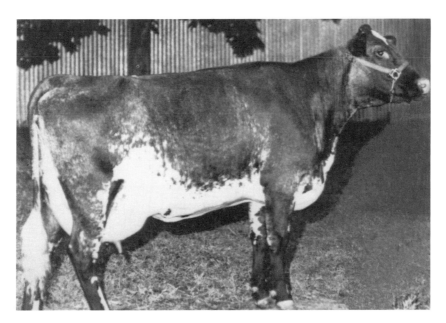

Kingsdale Lady Elegance 42nd holds many records for Milking Shorthorns.

MILKING SHORTHORN. "The Nation's Most Improved Dairy Breed" has a distinguished history. The Shorthorn breed originated hundreds of years ago in northeastern England in the valley of the Tees River. During the sixteenth century, there were short-horned cattle on the Yorkshire estates of England's nobility. These "English Shorthorns" were noted for their good milking qualities and ease of management. The Shorthorns that came to America in the late eighteenth century (often referred to as Durhams) furnished milk, meat, and power for the pioneers. The Illawarra Shorthorn of Australia has contributed greatly to the improvement of the breed.

The Milking Shorthorn is one of the most versatile of all cattle breeds. Females weigh over 2000 pounds and produce large quantities of milk—about 11,000 pounds per year. Calves not kept for breeding or milk production gain weight efficiently and provide excellent meat. An adult male averages about 2500 pounds.

RED POLL. Cattle raisers use the term "polled" to refer to stock with no horns. As the name of this breed implies, the Red Poll is hornless. The characteristic red coloring is found in virtually every member. A cow can also be distinguished from other breeds by its long legs and relatively small udder. Females weigh from 1200 to 1500 pounds; males average from 1800 to 2000 pounds.

Originally known as "The Red Polled Cattle Descended From The Norfolk And Suffolk Red Polled of England," members of this breed are considered to be dual-purpose cattle because they produce reasonably large quantities of milk and have good beef qualities. Red Polls were officially recognized as a distinct breed in 1846 and were brought to the United States in 1873. Today, they are found "from border to border and coast to coast."

RED DANISH. What produces about 9500 pounds of milk per year, comes from Denmark, and is red all over? Red Danish cattle are one of the youngest recognized dairy breeds, achieving this distinction in 1878. The first Red Danish cattle imported to the United States arrived in 1935. A mature Red Danish cow weighs about 1300 pounds; bulls weigh about 1800 pounds.

4

Working with Dairy Cattle

Most stock raisers agree that if you want an animal to produce for you, you've got to be good to it. This is especially true of cows. Some folks say that if you keep a cow contented, she'll try even harder to please you.

There once was a commercial on American television that advertised milk "from contented cows." No doubt these animals were outstanding producers that received extra special attention. The practice of treating exceptional milkers with tender loving care is still followed.

How people treat dairy cows varies from place to place. Regardless of location, a cow must have proper feeding, housing, and care to produce milk of consistent quality and quantity.

Feeding

Cattle must eat a balanced diet. Although the expression "fat as a cow" is often used to ridicule an overweight human, a fat dairy cow is undesirable. If fed too much, a cow gains weight

Above: Holstein cows receive alfalfa-grass supplementary feeding.
Below: Feeding silage from a tractor-pulled, power-driven feed wagon.

To produce milk, cows must consume large amounts of feed and water every day. This photo was taken in 1929.

Holstein calves in California are brought their daily ration of feed.

and is more expensive to keep. If fed too little, her production declines.

A number of factors influence the selection of dairy cattle feeds. These include balance of nutrients, bulkiness, and cost to the farmer. Likes and dislikes of individual cows are also taken into consideration.

On large farms, commercial feeds that are rich in protein are used. Many cows are fed the by-products of other industries, such as distillers' and brewers' grains from whiskey and beer making. On a number of small farms, cattle raisers grow their own feeds, supplementing the diet with seasonal vegetation or garden scraps.

Some feeds, such as wild onions, give milk a strange taste if they are eaten by cows just before milking time. Furthermore, cattle bloat if they eat too much alfalfa or green clover.

Livestock specialists say that bovines must have water twice daily. However, there is a lot of local tradition associated with the water requirement of dairy cows. Some farmers in tropical climates chill the water they give to their cows, based on the belief that cool water aids milk production in hot weather. Others in cold climates warm the water slightly, reinforcing the notion that warm water encourages milk production in frigid weather. Salt is important in all climates.

Housing

For many centuries, it was believed that livestock needed little or no protection from the elements. In parts of the world where human living conditions are poor, this practice is still followed. However, it is generally accepted that keeping cows warm and secure is necessary for good milk yield.

Shelters for cattle vary from one dairyland to another. A single-cow family often utilizes a small structure, with a window

Two views of dairy farms, one in Maryland (above) and one in Ohio. Note the barns, silos, and outbuildings.

to provide sunlight and air and a wide door to allow the cow easy passage when she is pregnant. An area for hay or grain storage is usually available. Space for the calf produced each year is also provided. Where different types of livestock are raised, a large building may be subdivided into individual stalls for cows, sheep, horses, or other animals. A huge dairy herd typically is housed in a barn designed for easy milking and handling.

The "conventional" dairy barn has a stall for each cow. The size of a stall differs from breed to breed. Pen-type barns permit cows to run loose in a large enclosed building, which is often referred to as the "loafing room."

Dairy bulls seldom pasture with cows. Males require a shelter and a pen that provide protection from the weather and a place to exercise. This is usually a box stall in a barn opening into a fenced area.

Care

Most of the care provided to dairy cattle is geared toward fostering a lifestyle that promotes milk production. Many governments provide tests for health maintenance and disease control. This involves a visit from a veterinarian who samples the udders of all cows on a particular farm for bacteria. When the test results are in, the veterinarian reviews them with the owner. Cows are innoculated with vaccines if necessary.

Control of mastitis, a disease responsible for a reduction in milk production, is essential on all dairy farms. In recent times, mastitis has become particularly troublesome due to the widespread use of milking machines, which often assist in spreading germs from one cow to another.

Other maladies that have plagued cows for centuries are brucellosis and tuberculosis. The former is a bacterial infection that causes pregnant cows to miscarry. The latter, which is also

Above: A truck is used to bring in the cows on this Minnesota dairy farm. Below: "Cowboys" herd cattle from pasture to milking barn in North Carolina.

Controlling disease among livestock is important in all parts of the world. These cattle are being sprayed at the Acholi Ranch, Uganda.

caused by germs, cripples the lungs and other organs. Both diseases can be transmitted to humans.

Keeping records on individual animals enables dairy farmers to monitor diseases and keep track of the efficiency of vaccinations and treatments. To assist in tracking milk yield and breeding performance, cows are marked for identification with ear tags, neck chains, tail tags, ear and udder tattoos, or brands.

Nature provided cattle with horns as a form of protection. Today, the horns are considered a characteristic of some breeds. However, in day-to-day dairying, horns present a safety hazard to the handler as well as allowing aggressive cows to intimidate or injure timid ones.

Dairy cows and bulls often have their horns removed when they are calves. This is done by clipping, sawing, or the use of caustic. The last method is considered to be the most humane since, with it, there is considerably less pain, infection, and death than with clipping or sawing. A ring is often put in a bull's nose so that he can be led more easily.

All cattle have four cloven hoofs, each hoof with two toes. If kept outdoors, these animals rarely need to have their toenails trimmed. If toes are allowed to grow too long, the hoofs lose their normal shape.

Good dairy cattle care includes understanding the personalities of individual animals and responding to their behavior. A great deal of attention must be given to heifers. Most of their naughtiness can be attributed to youth and vigor, which makes them very playful. They also lack the large udder that restricts the movement of their mothers. Many love to escape from their own pastures for a visit to heifers on other farms. Some like to dine on the vegetable gardens of neighboring homesteads. Observers note that heifers have a knack for determining when the grass is greener on the other side of the fence. As a result, many farmers keep their fences well maintained to prevent their valuable youngstock from wandering.

A winning smile reflects a blue ribbon at a fair in Essex Junction, Vermont. Note the ear tag (right ear) for identification.

5

"Milk for the Taking"

It has been said that milk is not "given" by cows. However, if you are "wily and strong and ruthless, you can have it for the taking."

Most people who work with dairy cattle for a living are satisfied if a cow yields sixty pounds of milk or more per day. That's enough to fill over a hundred glasses! The amount of butterfat content and number of live offspring (as well as *their* production records) are used to gauge the efficiency of a given animal.

A large number of people milk by hand—either out of necessity or because of the satisfaction derived from doing it yourself.

Milking by hand requires patience, perseverance, and persistence. The basic difficulty that must be overcome is that a cow's udder has four quarters while the milker has only two hands. The skill—knowing how to trap the milk in the teat with the thumb and index finger, how to prevent its return into the udder, how to force it out of the teat and into the pail—can only be acquired with experience.

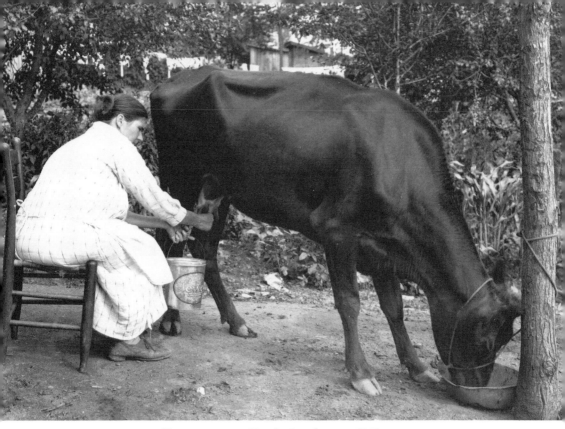

A farm woman milking a cow in North Carolina in 1929

The secret of successful milking by hand lies in getting a cow to "let down" her milk. This is usually the result of a series of activities such as providing a good meal, calm handling, washing the udder with warm water and a little bit of bleach, and drawing a few streams of milk from each teat to start the flow. If the milker performs these tasks with regularity, a cow becomes contented and lets her milk down on schedule.

From the cow's viewpoint, these "let down" activities release a hormone into the bloodstream that causes fibers to contract and force stored milk into the teat. When a cow is startled, frightened, or distracted, a hormone is produced that causes the flow of milk to stop. If this occurs, it may take twenty or thirty minutes before she can be milked.

To keep their cows contented, some farmers pipe in soft music, such as the type heard in elevators, doctors' offices, and department stores. Others create the appropriate atmosphere with bluegrass or classical music.

Since milking is a joint effort between man and beast, the amount of time it takes to milk a cow by hand is different from animal to animal and person to person. The average varies from ten to slightly more than thirty minutes per cow. An expert can milk as many as twelve cows in an hour!

Milk at the push of a button is commonplace on large commercial dairy operations. There are machines that draw milk from one cow after another at the rate of about one hundred cows per hour, shutting off when each is finished! Machine milking is typically done in a room called a milking parlor where cows are led into stalls and milked twice a day in assembly-line fashion. Some cows are milked three times daily.

Milking by machine is not without its own ritual. First, the cows' udders are washed. Next, they are dried. Then, the teats are attached to suction cups, which create a vacuum that simulates a sucking calf. Once the suction cups of the milking machine are attached, milk shoots into sterilized glass jars fastened to each cow's stall.

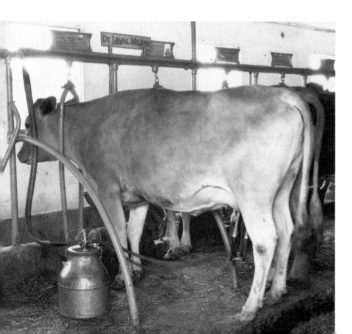

An early milking machine, Prince Georges County, Maryland, 1928

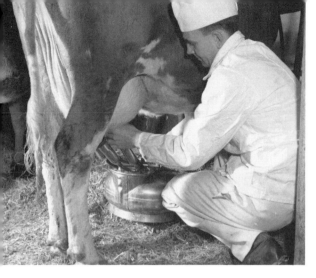

Left: Milking, early 1940's style

Right: Milking a cow at the Thai-German Dairy Farm at Chaing Mai, Thailand, 1973

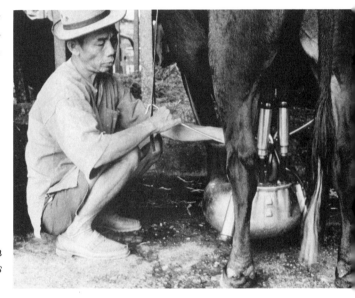

Below: On this farm in Alaska, milking machines are taken to the cows.

The temperature of milk when it leaves a cow's udder is about the same as the animal's body temperature—100° Fahrenheit. After it is collected in the jars, milk is piped to a tank in a nearby room. There it is cooled to 45° Fahrenheit or lower.

Each time cows are milked, the machines and the animals are washed. This is done to keep the milk clean and to prevent contamination. In commercial operations, no human hands ever come into contact with the milk.

When milking is completed, cows are herded into a holding barn next door to the milking parlor. Here, a snack of silage and grain usually awaits them.

People who sell the milk produced by their cows generally do so in bulk quantities to distributors or through cooperative agencies. These organizations typically handle the processing and distribution of bottled milk, cream, butter, ice cream, cheese, and other dairy products.

In the old days, if you wanted milk when you traveled, you had to take your cow with you. The Pilgrims brought cows to the New World, and pioneers in the United States and Australia did not leave their cows at home when they journeyed into unsettled territories. Even Admiral Richard E. Byrd, the famous explorer, took cows along when he went to the South Pole.

Today, you don't have to travel with a cow to have fresh milk. Thanks to modern production and delivery methods, milk is available almost everywhere.

Years ago, haulers with wagons traveled country roads to farms, collected milk in metal cans, and took it to local towns to be sold. A modern eighteen-wheeler refrigerated tank truck can hold about 52,000 pounds of milk! To meet the demand for milk and other dairy foods, the truckers who collect from small farms and large commercial operations are on the road seven days per week in all kinds of weather.

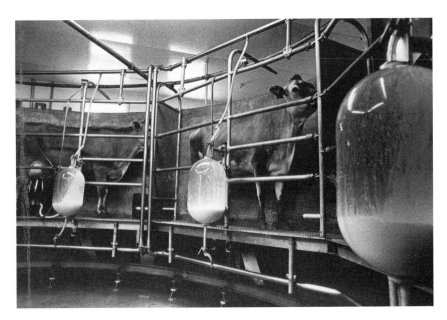

Above: An automated revolving milking parlor in South Carolina

Below: Maryland farmers watch the amount of milk given by their cows.

This milkman made his early-morning rounds in old St. Louis with a unique delivery set-up.

These dairy haulers who drive the backroads and highways are modern-day folk heroes. Stories are told of pickups and deliveries being made under all types of conditions—from blizzards and ice storms to hurricanes and week-long rains. But it is said that the greatest danger a hauler faces is going up a steep hill with a truck that is half full. When the weight of the milk shifts to the rear, the driver has all he can do to shift gears along with it! Most drivers compensate for this by filling the tank's front compartment first. This puts more weight over the wheels and helps balance the rig.

In many places, it is critical that milk be picked up as scheduled. This is because few in the milk business have what is called "margin"—extra space in their cooling tanks for an additional day's milking.

The milkman has also become a legendary figure famous for early morning deliveries of bottles of fresh milk and cream to homes and schools in all kinds of weather. In some parts of the world, he has been replaced by the dairy section of the local supermarket. In others, he continues to thrive.

6

"From *Mooo* to You"

Whole milk. Skim milk. Cream. Butter. Cheese. Buttermilk. Cream cheese.

A walk through the dairy department of any supermarket might make one think there are almost as many products made from milk as there are cows producing it. Rest assured, this is not the case. There are millions of cows making milk: only several hundred products are made from it.

Few people today worry about whether or not the dairy products they buy are safe to eat. This wasn't always the case. For centuries, intestinal disorders were caused by so-called "bad" milk, butter, or cheese. Then, in 1856, French chemist and bacteriologist Louis Pasteur (1822–1895) discovered that milk right out of the cow contains germs that can cause illness in humans. Fortunately, Pasteur's experiments also revealed that heat kills these germs. Ever since then, milk has been heated—pasteurized—to make it safe for human consumption.

Here's a brief look at some of the products made from the milk of dairy cattle.

Today milk travels in sanitary eighteen-wheelers. Would you rather have the milk this tank truck holds (38,000 pounds) or the milk this cow gives in a year? Pick the cow—she gave 50,759 pounds in 1974. That's nearly 24,000 quarts.

Milk

Milk comes in bottles and cartons that bear its name in big bold letters and probably does more for the human body than any other beverage. Statistics are the best indication of the popularity of milk—over 42 million gallons are delivered to cities and towns in America each and every day! Consumption of milk is also high in Great Britain, Canada, and Australia. And the demand for it continues to grow.

Commercial milk is sold in several forms. Whole milk con-

The milk pouring from the cow into this receiver jar is raw.

tains four percent butterfat. It is also distributed as a "lowfat" product with a content of one or two percent butterfat. Skim milk has only half the caloric content of whole milk because the butterfat has been removed. The term "homogenized" is applied to milk that has had the fat globules broken up and distributed throughout.

Evaporated milk is canned whole milk that has had about half of its water removed. Condensed milk, which is also sold in cans, has had its water content reduced by about 60 percent. Powdered or "dry" milk (which may be whole or skim) has had 95 percent of its moisture removed.

Whether or not a person ever outgrows the need for milk depends on individual nutritional requirements. Nevertheless, it is worth mentioning that this food is an excellent source of calcium, riboflavin, phosphorus, and other minerals. As a major contributor of protein to the human diet, it also supplies numerous vitamins including A, D, and E.

Milk advertisements generally focus on its health benefits, natural ingredients, and pleasant taste. As a refreshment, many people feel milk is best served cold. Some like it hot—plain or mixed with a little cocoa. The common belief that warmed milk helps one sleep is not without basis in fact. Scientists have determined that there are several ingredients in milk that, when heated, aid the slumber process.

Curds and whey, the favorite dish of Little Miss Muffet, are made from congealed milk. Curds are somewhat solid; whey is thin and watery. Buttermilk is made from pasteurized skim milk that has had a culture added to develop flavor and consistency.

Long life is often attributed to a diet including large quantities of naturally soured and fermented milk. Fanciers of yogurt, which is made from milk curdled by the action of cultures, swear by its great taste, nutritional value, and legendary link with longevity. Some people love it the first time they try it. Others say a yearning for yogurt must be acquired.

It would take an enormous cookbook to list all of the recipes utilizing milk. A key ingredient in custards, cakes, cookies, candies, casseroles, and a collection of other concoctions, milk is a popular cooking component throughout the world.

Cream

Common speech has provided the expression "Cream rises to the top," descriptive of people who excel above all others. Similarly, the phrase "Cream of the crop" refers to the best. When milk is left standing, cream (the part of milk rich in butterfat) rises by itself to the surface of a container.

In some parts of the world, cream is skimmed off the top of its container by hand. Commercial operations and small farms generally obtain cream from milk by using a centrifuge, a machine that rotates at high speed and separates substances according to density.

Cream has a sweet taste, rich texture, and a slightly off-white or yellowish color. Its butterfat content ranges from 10 to 70 percent. Most household (light) cream contains from 18 to 25 percent butterfat; some has up to 32 percent. Heavy cream is 40 percent butterfat. When air is beaten in or when charged with carbon dioxide, cream forms a foam called "whipped" cream. "Sour" cream, as the name implies, has been allowed to turn sour.

A number of dairy foods are made from cream. Cream soup refers to any puree made with cream. Ice cream is a frozen food consisting of cream, sugar, and various flavors. Clotted cream, a popular spread for scones in Great Britain, is produced by scalding and cooling. Cream sauce is a white sauce consisting of cream, flour, and butter. But there is no cream in cream soda!

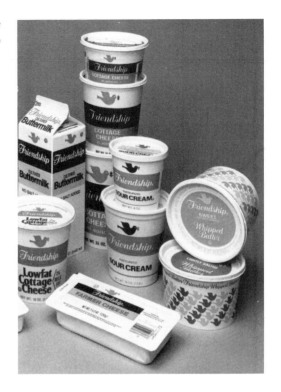

The word "cream" is applied to thick liquids used as medication as well as soft-centered confections or fudge coated with chocolate. "Creamy" is applied to anything having the color or texture of cream. However, when people ask for cereal cream, they usually want the cream of milk.

Butter

In the old days, butter was made for family use by pouring heated sweet or soured cream into a barrel churn and "churning" it for hours. If there was more than the family could use, it was sold in the local village, providing a source of income. No doubt the phrase "bread and butter," which refers to how an individual earns his livelihood, is derived from this practice.

The young people of America do their part in getting milk and its products onto the country's tables. This young boy has no trouble milking the cow but considerable difficulty finding the pail with the stream of milk.

By law, all of the butter sold in the United States must have more than 80 percent fat content. Salt is sometimes added for flavor or as a preservative. Yellow coloring, which serves no purpose other than to give this food visual appeal, is often included during processing. Incidentally, the word "creamery," which is found on many butter packages, is a holdover from the practice of sending cream to a place called a creamery for processing.

Cheese

Although the milk of sheep, goats, and other animals is suit-

A teen-age girl lines up the cows for milking. Chores—sometimes deadly dull, physical, but absolutely necessary—are a big part of farm life, especially for youngsters.

able for producing this dairy product, most cheese is made from cow's milk.

A complete discussion of cheese would require a book much larger than this. However, it is worth noting that cheese may be hard or soft, depending on the amount of water left in it and the way it is made. Individual flavor, which ranges from sharp and tangy to mild and bland, depends on how the cheese was ripened. The saying "Cheese is milk's leap toward immortality" is based on this food's ability to be preserved for long periods of time.

Some popular cheeses made from cow's milk are Cheddar, Swiss, Gouda, and Muenster. Cottage cheese (often called

Dutch cheese) is made by allowing skim milk to sour until it is thoroughly curdled. Cream cheese, made from cream or sweet milk, is soft, white, and smooth textured. Creamed cottage cheese is made by adding sweet or sour cream to cottage cheese.

At one time, cheese making was a domestic operation conducted on individual farms. In Europe, the manufacture of cheese is a source of national pride and competition within and among countries. American dairy corporations and cottage operations produce over a billion pounds a year for cheese lovers in the United States. But no matter how you slice it, cheese is a favorite food all over the world.

Dairy Beef and Veal

Milk is not the only product obtained from dairy cattle. Beef was once considered to be a by-product of the dairy industry. With the growing demand for low cholesterol foods, dairy cattle have become a valuable source of lean beef. Cows that produce less than the average amount of milk for their breed or individuals that no longer yield large quantities are removed from the herd (a process called culling) and butchered for their meat. Old bulls are sent to market when they are considered to be of no value as breeding stock. Incidentally, the hides of cattle sold to the slaughterhouse are often used to make leather goods.

Veal, the flesh of milk-fed calves that are at least three weeks old, is another by-product of the dairy industry. Vealers are usually bull calves that are not kept for breeding. Most of the veal sold in the United States, Great Britain, and other countries comes from Holstein, Ayrshire, Brown Swiss, and Milking Shorthorn calves.

Famous Dairy Cattle

Billions and billions of dairy cattle have walked the earth. The vast majority have served man without recognition, their names spoken only by the farmers and families who kept them.

But not all dairy cattle are "unknowns." Some purebreds have achieved notoriety on the basis of their accomplishments as milk producers. Others are famous for being sold at auction for record sums.

The careers of outstanding individuals are closely watched by people involved in the dairy cattle business. Breed associations keep a record of every registered purebred in a volume known as the Herdbook. In addition to the official name of the individual animal, this record usually includes the names of the owner, breeder, sire, and dam, as well as a registration or tattoo number and the animal's birth date.

Here are some of the most famous dairy cattle:

Kingsdale Lady Elegance 42D 373844 holds many of the National Champion Records for Milking Shorthorns. As of 1985, she was considered to be the breed's top milk producer. Another "meritorious cow" is Clayside Cinderella 2d 347863, who yielded 103,220 pounds of milk in her lifetime and produced three excellent daughters as well as an outstanding son.

One of the most famous Holsteins is Zeldenhurst Pontiac Korndyke, who produced 306,051 pounds of milk and 11,649 pounds of butterfat in her lifetime. Another well-known Holstein is Pabst Sir Roburke Rag Apple, who sired 3067 daughters.

Among the Ayrshires, Crusader's Joyce of Windy Top is famous for her lifetime output of 206,888 pounds of milk and 8725 pounds of butterfat. When she was twenty years old, she produced 13,122 pounds of milk and 630 pounds of butterfat in 305 days. She was milked twice per day during that period. Oak Ridge Kelly's Rosid, known as "Big Red," was an all-breed

Oak Ridge Kelly's Rosid, a champion Ayrshire until her death in 1977

Selwood Betty's Commander, a famous Ayrshire bull

champion until her death in 1977. Selwood Betty's Commander, who died in 1969, was famous for his ability to sire outstanding daughters.

Century Acres Liz C. has been a world's record holder for milk production by a Brown Swiss cow. In 356 days, she gave 38,440 pounds of milk and 1695 pounds of butterfat. Another outstanding member of this breed, Schulte's Sunwise Pat, has been nominated for the All American-cow award five times. Idyl Wild Improver Jinx 664521 was sold for a record price at a public auction in 1983.

Brown Swiss Idyl Wild Improver Jinx brought record 1983 auction price.

Guernsey Cleverlands Darimost Chrystal, star of the World Dairy Expo

Cleverlands Darimost Chrystal was the First Guernsey Supreme Champion at the World Dairy Expo. Another Guernsey, Ideal's Superior, is recognized as a Gold Star Sire, having fathered 182 daughters that have averaged 12,556 pounds of milk per year and 689 pounds of butterfat. Welcome Choice Admiral is now the breed's most active bull.

Welcome Choice Admiral is the Guernsey breed's most active bull.

Munifordia's Oxfordia 4th was a Champion Milk Producer for 1973–74, 1976–78, and 1980. She was the Jersey breed's first 200,000-pound milk cow.

The Jersey breed has had many other notable members. In 1919, a bull named Sybil's Gamboge was sold at auction in the United States for $65,000, an enormous sum at the time. According to the Royal Jersey Agricultural and Horticultural Society, this amount stood as a record for sixty years, and "in real financial terms has never been equalled."

A number of Jersey cows have been bestowed on British royalty. La Sente's Miss Beonzemine, a "splendid specimen of the breed," was presented to His Majesty King George V in 1921. Queen Elizabeth II received Beauchamp Oxford Lady during a visit to the island in 1957. Twenty-one years later, she was given another lovely Jersey named Ansom Designette.

Centuries ago, primitive peoples made drawings of cattle, thinking this would ensure a steady flow of milk. Today, images of cows are used on containers and packages, as well as in advertisements for all types of diary products. None are as famous as Elsie the Cow, mascot and trademark of Borden, Inc.

Elsie was originally launched as a cartoon character in medical journals during the 1930's. At the time, she co-starred with other cartoon cows, including Mrs. Blossom, Bessie, and Clara. In 1938, Elsie came to life in a radio series of milk commercials featuring letters "written" by her to news commentator Rush Hughes. The radio Elsie caught on with the public. She started receiving more fan mail than Mr. Hughes! Gradually her popularity grew to the point where a *real* Elsie was needed.

Her first appearance in the flesh was at the 1939 New York World's Fair. A beautiful seven-year-old purebred Jersey cow named You'll Do, Lobelia was dressed in an embroidered green blanket for millions of fairgoers to see.

In a short time, Elsie the Cow became a national celebrity,

appearing in magazines and motion pictures. She was joined by a Jersey bull who became known as "Elmer." He has been used in advertisements for Borden's white glue. Elsie/Lobelia toured the country with her real daughter, Beulah, until the former met an untimely death in a truck accident in 1940.

A new Jersey cow named Noble Aim Standard became the second living Elsie in 1940. She earned honorary degrees such as Doctor of Bovinity and Doctor of Ecownomics from various universities.

During this same period, Elsie's cartoon image evolved into "a happy mixture of cow and your average young housewife." Not only could she talk, but the 1940's Elsie could stand upright!

The cartoon Elsie, Borden's trademark, and her son Beauregard

Both the live and the cartoon Elsie added a new family member in 1947. Son Beauregard replaced Beulah as her traveling companion. Later, the live Elsie gave birth to twins (a rare event for bovines) who were named Larabee and Lobelia but are often referred to simply as The Twins.

During the fifties and sixties, the cartoon Elsie fell on hard times, partially due to Borden, Inc.'s, need to project a different type of corporate image. Furthermore, the costs associated with a traveling Elsie Show had increased tremendously.

However, the early 1970's saw a rebirth of the cartoon Elsie in television commercials. A new live Elsie (real name: "Cricket") was recruited in Ohio in 1971. Elsie/Cricket (who was too much of a family pet to go on the road) was replaced in 1972 by Goldie. This Jersey cow is considered by many to be "the prettiest Elsie there has ever been." Today, Elsie the Cow ranks as one of the most widely recognized corporate symbols in the world—and heads the list of famous dairy cattle!

Elsie the Cow, most famous of all dairy cattle

Index